DRUGS
THE COMPLETE STORY

ALCOHOL

Pamela Holmes

STECK-VAUGHN
LIBRARY
A Division of Steck-Vaughn Company

Austin, Texas

CONTENTS

CONTENTS

GLOSSARY

addiction: the forming of a dependence on alcohol.
alcoholic: someone who is addicted to alcohol.
Alcoholics Anonymous: a large self-help group for alcoholics, which has helped thousands of people. Al-Anon Family Groups provide support to the families of alcoholics.
congeners: the hundreds of flavor substances used in the various types of alcohol.
connoisseur: someone who is an expert on wines, their taste, and country of origin.
cooper: someone who makes or repairs wooden tubs and barrels.
dehydration: the loss of water from the body, often caused by taking alcohol.
distillation: the method by which alcohol is made purer by being heated beyond the point at which fermentation stops. The alcohol is collected as vapor.
fetal alcohol syndrome: babies born with birth defects because their mothers consumed alcohol during pregnancy.
intoxication: the effects of drinking too much alcohol.
liquor: a distilled alcohol, such as whiskey, gin, or vodka.
mash: the starchy mixture from which alcohol can be distilled or brewed.
Surgeon General: the chief American medical officer for health.
teetotaler: someone who does not drink any alcohol.
toxic: poisonous.

1

OUR MOST USED DRUG

Ask a man or woman in the street if they take drugs, and they are likely to assure you that they do not. However, if they drink alcohol, smoke cigarettes, or drink coffee, their reply will be incorrect. The alcohol in drinks, the nicotine in tobacco, and the caffeine in coffee and tea are all drugs. They are substances on which the body and/or mind can come to depend — in other words, substances to which they can become addicted.

Unlike drugs such as heroin and cocaine, alcohol, nicotine, and caffeine are "socially acceptable" drugs. This means that in most countries no one will be put in prison if they simply drink alcohol or coffee or smoke cigarettes. However, all drugs have an effect on the body, mind, emotions, and life of the person who takes them.

Many people who drink alcohol only have a little, enjoying the relaxing effect alcohol has on them and their behavior. They would say that alcohol adds to their lives, that drinking alcohol is pleasurable and something they enjoy.

Alcohol is the most widely used drug in the world.

Other people who cannot control their drinking can find that their lives are ruined by their addiction to or dependence on alcohol. They become unable to resist drinking large quantities of the drug, which is legally and freely available. They may have been encouraged to drink by advertisements that often promote the use of alcohol as a glamorous social activity. The casual way in which society treats alcohol can sometimes

5

discourage alcoholics from recognizing their addiction and delay them from getting help.

Alcohol is the most widely used drug in the world. It is consumed all over the world except in countries such as Saudi Arabia where the national religion bans the drinking of alcohol. Countries have very varied social customs and traditions that involve drinking alcohol. In France and Italy, for example, alcohol is traditionally taken with meals. In other countries, alcohol is drunk on special occasions, to celebrate weddings, anniversaries, and important events.

> *Today, both men and women are drinking at younger ages, in greater quantities, more often, and in a wider number of social settings, inside and outside the home.*

Today, both men and women are drinking at younger ages, in greater quantities, more often, and in a wider number of social settings. People all over the world are now drinking beer, wine, and spirits rather than traditionally brewed drinks such as mead and rice wine. At one time, many people grew their own

Alcohol is often drunk when people gather together for celebrations or festivals, as in this beer-hall in Bavaria, Germany.

vegetables, raised animals, and chopped wood for fuel. They also made their own alcohol to drink. However, today, big business controls most alcohol production, distribution, and sales in both developed and developing countries.

Alcohol in history

According to myth, Noah planted the first vineyard after the flood and started to make wine. According to experts who study early civilizations, alcohol has been consumed for centuries. Egyptian stone reliefs from about 5000 B.C. depict the process of brewing ale from barley. Evidence has also been found on Rhum, an island off the northern coast of Scotland. The remains of a farming community of about 2000 B.C. included pots that contained traces of ale made from heather, fern spores, meadowsweet, and herbs. In about 1770 B.C., the Babylonians established a code of law to control the drinking of alcohol in "drinking houses."

Alcohol has been used throughout history in various ways. Some civilizations worshiped alcohol as a source of "good" : Osiris was an Egyptian god of wine, and the Romans worshiped their own god of wine, Bacchus. Alcohol became part of many

Wine was widely drunk in Roman times and even had its own god, Bacchus. He is shown here on the side of a Roman tomb pouring wine into a bowl.

rituals, and even today in Christian services, wine is used to represent the blood of Christ.

Alcohol has long been a part of social gatherings. By the Middle Ages, it was customary to offer alcohol at births, marriages, deaths, and the signing of treaties. In some countries, alcohol became part of the staple diet. It is a rich source of calories and may contain some vitamins and minerals. From the seventeenth century, farm workers and sailors would receive part of their wages in the form of alcohol, usually cider or rum. In many countries, water was contaminated and unsafe to drink. This meant that in the period before safe water supplies were introduced, it was preferable to drink alcohol.

> *It is said that prescriptions for beer were written by Sumerian doctors on clay tablets more than 4,000 years ago.*

Alcohol has been used as a medicine in many cultures. It is said that prescriptions for beer were written by Sumerian doctors on clay tablets more than 4,000 years ago. Even today, sherry or port may be used to encourage the appetites of elderly people. Alcohol was used to knock people out prior to operations before general anesthetics were developed. It was also used as an antiseptic to clean wounds before doctors understood what caused infection.

Religion and alcohol

Religion has influenced attitudes toward alcohol. The Aztec people considered alcohol a gift from the gods, and worshipers were expected to get intoxicated, but not drunk, on certain holy days. The Islamic religion bans the drinking of alcohol, and even today those found disobeying this holy law may be beaten or imprisoned.

The Catholic church has always been more tolerant than the Protestant church in its attitude toward drinking. This is probably because the seat of the Catholic religion is in Italy where the milder climate favors grape-growing and wine is part of the diet.

During the eighteenth century, the Protestants of northern Europe saw in their industrialized towns how drinking could

During the period of Prohibition in the 1920s smuggling illegal alcohol was common. These state troopers were photographed on their way to destroy a captured load.

affect people badly. The members of some branches of the Protestant church stopped drinking altogether and became teetotalers, their leaders preaching against the "curse of drink." The U.S., Norway, Finland, Sweden, and Canada, all largely Protestant countries, had bans on alcohol in the 1920s. The most famous of all these campaigns began in the United States in 1919. This "Prohibition" succeeded in ceasing the legal manufacturing of alcohol, and alcohol consumption did go down. However, it also created a black market for alcohol that led to an increase in activity and profit of organized crime in the U. S. Prohibition also made criminals out of otherwise law-abiding citizens, who broke the law by drinking alcohol. Prohibition was ended in 1933.

BREWING UP

If you stand any watery mixture of vegetable sugars or starches in a warm place for long enough, alcohol will start to form. This is undoubtedly how people first learned to make their own alcohol. Since that time, this "accident" has been refined, and today more sophisticated methods are used to make alcohol, but the basic principle is the same.

> *Alcohol is a colorless, flammable liquid with a characteristic smell and a strong taste.*

Yeast is used to ferment or cause a chemical reaction in certain sugars, such as the juice of the grape or the grain of a cereal crop like barley. The gas carbon dioxide is produced by this process, giving beer its "head" and champagne its sparkle. The yeast will go on fermenting the sugars and producing alcohol until the alcoholic content of the mixture reaches 14 percent. Yeast cells cannot live in an environment of more than 14 percent alcohol, and so fermentation stops.

The proper name for alcohol is ethyl alcohol. It is a colorless, flammable liquid with a characteristic smell and a strong taste.

Beer

The basic ingredients of beer are water, cereal (usually barley), hops, and yeast. First, the barley is malted, or mixed with water. This encourages the little kernels of barley to sprout, or germinate. This breaks down the starch in the hard husk of the

These copper vats are used for the fermentation of yeast and starch in cereals when making beer, utilizing a process that has been used for over 2,000 years. This brewery is in Germany.

cereal so that it becomes soluble in water. Yeast is then able to ferment the starch. The malting also gives beer its characteristic taste, color, and "body."

The process of germination is stopped by drying the mixture in a kiln. Then it is mixed with hot water to make a sweet brown liquid known as wort. This process is very like that of brewing a pot of tea. The wort is mixed with hops and boiled for several hours. When it has cooled, yeast is added to the mixture and fermentation begins. Gradually, alcohol is produced. The beer is siphoned off into casks, kegs, bottles, or cans. A glass of beer contains between three and five percent alcohol.

The same basic beer-making process has been used by brewers for over 2,000 years, although these days brewing is more sophisticated. The brewing process is scientifically controlled. Worldwide there are about 580 million barrels of beer brewed every year.

The beer market for low-calorie, low-alcohol beers is growing quickly today. These beers have escalated in sales since 1975 when light beers began to be enthusiastically promoted. Low-alcohol beer is made in the same way as the alcoholic type but the alcohol is taken out at the end of the process. Scientists are trying to find ways to make these new beers taste as similar as possible to the traditional brew.

> *The same basic beer-making process has been used by brewers for over 2,000 years, although these days brewing is more sophisticated.*

The light-colored beer, lager, is also an increasingly popular drink. It is made in a similar way to the darker beers, but a different yeast is used. The resulting drink is lighter in color.

The U.S. is the biggest brewer of beer in the world, followed by Germany, the Soviet Union, and the United Kingdom.

This modern brewery is in Malawi. The beer-making process is scientifically controlled so that huge quantities can be produced.

Grapevines cover the hillside in this German wine-growing region. Many acres of grapes are harvested in autumn, to be turned into a variety of wines.

Wine

Wine can be made from almost anything, for example root vegetables such as potatoes or parsnips, rice (as in Japan), and flowers. However, the drink that is known best by that name is made from the juice of crushed grapes. The juice is left in a warm place to ferment. Yeast changes the sugar in the juice into alcohol.

If all the natural sugar in the grape is turned into alcohol, the wine is "dry." If fermentation is stopped early, the wine still contains some unfermented sugar and so tastes "sweet." The carbon dioxide produced in the fermentation process is allowed to bubble away. A glass of wine is about 11 percent alcohol.

The white, red, or rosé (pink) color of wine is not the result of using a red- or white-fleshed grape. It depends on whether the skin of the grape is used. If the grape skins are removed from the fermenting liquid, the wine will be white. If the skins are left in the liquid, the wine will be red. Rosé wine is a mixture of both.

ALCOHOL

Champagne is a blend of several white wines that are fermented together for a second time in a firmly corked bottle so that none of the carbon dioxide bubbles escape. This gives the drink its "fizz." Sparkling wines are produced in the same way.

For many years, France was considered to be the leader in wine production. However, Italy, Spain, and Germany are also important wine producers. California, New York State, and Australian wines are becoming well-known and respected. Today, many people are going back to making their own wines, substituting other ingredients for grapes.

Spirits

Making spirits involves a process that is thought to have been discovered in about A.D. 600 by an Arabian physician who called spirits the "true water of life." In nature, the process of fermentation stops at 14 percent because the yeast cannot survive beyond this point. To get purer alcohol, the liquid that is left after fermentation must be heated. Since alcohol boils at a lower temperature than water, it escapes as a vapor or gas, leaving behind the water and juice in which it was mixed. This vapor is then caught in a cooling tube called a spirit receiver, where it condenses and turns back into liquid alcohol. The process is called distillation.

In the case of whiskey, the main ingredients used are malted barley (malting is the process used in making beer) and water. The malted barley is placed in a kiln and heated to stop it from germinating. The smoke from the kiln drifts up through the barley to dry it. In the case of Scotch whiskey, peat is added to the fuel in the kiln. The consequent peaty aroma gives the whiskey its distinctive taste.

The dried malted barley is ground to a "mash." Water and yeast are added, and the process of fermentation starts. Gradually the starch in the barley grain is converted into alcohol. Then the process of distillation takes place. The liquid is heated in huge copper vats. Copper is used because other metals would combine with the alcohol and alter its flavor.

The colorless alcohol is put into oak casks and stored in a cool, dark place where it remains for several years. During this time, the taste of the spirit improves. In Scotland, by law whiskey must mature for three years, but sometimes the spirit is left to sit for five or ten years or more. If it is stored in oak

Whiskey is siphoned into oak casks where it will mature for at least three years. The best whiskies are matured for over 10 years.

oak casks that have formerly been used for sherry, the whiskey will become a darker color than if it is stored in white oak casks.

A "shot" of whiskey has about 40 percent alcohol. Just under 80 million gallons of pure alcohol are distilled each year in Scotland in the form of Scotch whiskey. There are two main kinds of Scotch whiskey, namely malt and grain, and they differ in taste. Almost 80 percent of all Scotch whiskey is sold abroad. The U.S. is the largest export market (about 15.5 million gallons), followed by Japan (3.8 million gallons), and Australia (2.25 million gallons).

Whiskey is distilled and matured in several countries other than Scotland, such as Ireland, Brazil, Canada, and the U.S. Rye whiskey is made both in the U.S. and Canada and must be produced by a grain mash which is 51 percent rye grain. Bourbon is made from 51 percent corn grain and is made only in the U.S. It has to be matured for at least two years in white oak barrels that have been charred on the inside. The charring of the oak casks gives the distinctive flavoring and color to bourbon.

ALCOHOL

Distillation can produce a liquid with an alcoholic content of up to 93 percent. There are many different spirits produced around the world by this process. Vodka, a drink of Russian origin, was formerly distilled from fermented wheat mash. Today, it is also made from a mash of rye, wheat, or potatoes. Rum is made from fermented sugarcane. To produce a good light rum the liquid has to rest for six months in oak.

> *Distillation can produce a liquid with an alcoholic content of up to 93 percent.*

Gin is a distillation of rye, barley, or other grains which is then flavored with juniper berries. Other berries, such as sloe, can be used to flavor the gin instead of juniper. Brandy is distilled from wine or fermented fruit juice, while Calvados is a kind of brandy made by "burning" cider in a still.

3

THE BOOM INDUSTRY

The alcohol industry is a big employer. It is difficult to establish an exact figure of all the people who are involved in the making, distribution, marketing, and selling of alcohol in a country. However, it is estimated that about two million people in the U.S. and 1.5 million people in the U.K. earn their living from the alcohol industry.

Takeovers and growth

At one time, most alcohol was produced by small companies— local breweries, vineyards, or distilleries. However, over the last 30 years, the manufacture and selling of beer, wine, and spirits has become big business, involving multinational companies, huge amounts of money, and vast profits. In 1988, U.S. consumers spent over $88 billion on alcoholic drinks.

> *Mergers happen because it can be cheaper to run one big company than two.*

The alcohol industry began to develop rapidly after World War II. As the economies of the developed countries such as the U.S., U.K., and Australia improved and people had more money in their pockets, the demand for alcohol increased. The alcohol manufacturers expanded their businesses to match this demand.

In many cases, this expansion involved the merging of several small companies into one larger company. Mergers happen because it is usually cheaper to run one big company than two smaller ones. For example, only one administrative section is needed to organize wages and salaries. Systems that the big company has already developed can be used by the smaller one, in particular the distribution networks that the bigger company has already established.

Beginning in 1960 there was a dramatic fall in the number of brewing companies across the world. For example, in the U.S. there had been 171 companies in 1960; by 1980, there were only 43. In 1960 in Australia, there were 11 breweries but by 1980 only seven were left. The U.K. lost 166 breweries during the same period.

Knowing how to market one addictive product (tobacco) has given industry the needed experience for marketing another (alcohol).

In the past, when one business has bought up another, it has usually been in the same line of work. For example, a wine company might buy into another vineyard. However, this pattern has changed over the last 20 years. Companies have begun to move into other areas of business. There are advantages to this approach. The big "parent" company can afford to pump a lot of money into the "baby" company and help it to grow successfully. In 1969, the tobacco company

Guinness is very popular in Nigeria where this poster is displayed. A number of breweries market their beers in developing countries.

Philip Morris bought a small U.S. brewery, Miller. By 1980, Miller had become the world's second biggest brewer of beer.

There is evidence that the tobacco companies that have been successful in selling cigarettes to developing countries have marketed alcohol using similar methods. Knowing how to market one addictive product (tobacco) has given industry the needed experience for marketing another (alcohol).

Selling alcohol in the developing world is big business.

This raises a moral question. Many developing countries are in massive debt to international banks. Is it right that so much of their limited national income is being spent on goods such as tobacco and alcohol which are nonessential and a risk to health? Particularly when it is often the countries of those very banks that promote the consumption of alcohol because it can bring their governments additional income in the form of taxes.

Reaching out

In the 1970s there was a worldwide economic slowdown. The rise in oil prices had a bad effect on business everywhere. The alcohol companies needed to find new markets where they could sell more of their product. Many looked to the developing countries and realized that there were vast numbers of people there who did not buy much alcohol. Improved systems of communication and transportation meant that it was easier to reach the developing countries. Today, selling alcohol in the developing world is big business.

. . . this was a way of showing their friends and colleagues that they were successful and had sophisticated international tastes.

At the same time, within those countries, there was a general drift of people from the rural areas into the cities, where the populations grew enormously. Some of these were unskilled people looking for work, while others found employment in new business concerns. Many adopted a Western way of life,

ALCOHOL

As more sophisticated vehicles and machines are developed, it has become easier for breweries to distribute their beers at home and abroad.

part of which included the regular drinking of alcohol. They abandoned traditionally made drinks and more often chose beer, wine, or spirits. If they could afford to buy imported spirits, this was a way of showing their friends and colleagues that they were successful and had sophisticated international tastes. Governments also realized that a lot of money could be made from the taxes and duties charged on alcoholic drinks.

Some of the multinational alcohol companies started to export liquor to developing countries. Others set up breweries and distilleries within the countries themselves. Between 1975 and 1980, of the 46 countries where beer output grew by about 50 percent, 42 were developing countries. Most of the beer is consumed locally.

Big business affects how alcohol is sold. Many liquor stores are situated in the same shopping center as supermarkets, making it easier for the shopper. Rows and rows of attractive bottles are displayed featuring alcohol for every taste: sophisticated and expensive wines and champagne, exotic liqueurs, distilled spirits, imported and domestic beers, and wine coolers. Shopping carts are also provided to help the shopper make big purchases.

In some states, such as Florida and Texas, people can buy alcohol in supermarkets. They are attracted by the cut-rate prices and convenience of one-stop shopping. Supermarkets can buy, ship, and even bottle the wines they sell, thus making them cheaper for the customer. In other states, such as New Jersey, alcohol can only be purchased in liquor stores.

A family concern?

The distilleries where Scotch whiskey is made have traditionally been built in rural areas close to where the ingredients needed to make it are plentiful. The distillery can be a good source of employment for local people. Within one family, father and son may even work at the same distillery.

If the industry goes through a bad economic period and workers are laid off, a pocket of unemployment develops. Where the distillery is a local business, there may be several members of one family unemployed at the same time. In the late 1970s, sales of whiskey peaked and then fell because of an

In Scotland, small whiskey distilleries are still common, such as this one at Fort William. Often many local people depend on the distillery for work.

economic recession. Twelve out of 130 distilleries in Scotland had to close and many people lost their jobs. It was not only the distillery workers who became unemployed. The effects of the closures were also felt, indirectly, by farmers who had grown the barley, people working in transportation, coopers who made the wooden casks in which whiskey is matured, and coppersmiths who made the copper vats. The closures therefore had a widespread effect on the local community.

4

DRINKING TOO MUCH

Alcohol is a drug that is taken in many different countries. Except in Muslim countries and in "dry" areas within countries where consumption is forbidden, like Saudi Arabia, alcohol is being drunk in greater quantities every year.

Consumption

When people are asked how much they drink, they probably say "not much." Research has shown that drinkers nearly always underestimate the amount they drink. It is possible to get a more accurate record by asking them to keep a drink diary and to note every time they have a drink. It often comes as a shock to the diarist to find out how much they are actually drinking.

> *Research has shown that drinkers nearly always underestimate the amount they drink.*

In the U.K., about one in nine Britons is drinking over a bottle of wine, or four pints of beer, or a third of a bottle of spirits every day. This is way above the maximum recommended by doctors. On an international table showing per-person consumption, Britain came in the bottom half immediately below the U.S. France tops the table, with Australia coming about halfway down it. The table also revealed that the French and Germans consume nearly twice as much alcohol as Americans.

Over the past 30 years, there has been a big increase in the amount of alcohol consumed in the U.S., Europe, Australia,

ALCOHOL

Canada, and New Zealand. A similar pattern is being seen in developing countries, although at lower levels than in the West. This rise peaked in the late 1970s and there has been a slight drop in consumption since then. However, people are still drinking more than is good for their health. It has been estimated that there are about ten million alcoholics and 90 million other drinkers in the U.S. alone.

Alcohol has a bad effect on health. There has been a sharp increase in the number of deaths from cirrhosis of the liver, that is, a "fatty" liver that does not work well. The liver is responsible for breaking down the alcohol in the body. There has also been an increase in admissions to psychiatric units and mental hospitals for alcoholism, drunkenness, drunk-driving arrests, and other alcohol-related incidents such as spouse abuse, violence, and accidents.

Why do we drink?

Drinking habits are not fixed. Within each country and over a period of time, levels of drinking change. They are influenced by several factors.

Alcohol plays a major part in causing road accidents. Drivers who have been drinking are less capable of driving properly.

There is a link between a country's standard of living and how much alcohol the people of that country consume. When there are economic hardships, people tend to drink less. For example, in the depression of the 1930s when millions were unemployed, alcohol consumption fell. There is also a link between the cost of alcohol and how much people drink. By adjusting the price through taxes and duties, a government can control the amount of alcohol that people drink.

> *There is a link between a country's standard of living and how much alcohol the people of that country consume.*

Government policies on drinking can also affect consumption. In the Soviet Union, the government has tried to restrict drinking by cutting down on the amount of alcohol produced. They also put restrictions on where people can buy it. In the past ten years, there has been a fall in the amount of alcohol that is drunk in several other countries, including France. A government-sponsored campaign has encouraged parents not to give their children under 14 years any alcoholic drink, and then to offer only wine diluted with water to teenagers. The advertising of spirits is also banned on French television and at the cinemas.

The social attitude toward drinking has an impact as well. In the nineteenth century when excessive drinking in the U.K. caused public drunkenness, family quarrels, and ill-health, several anti-alcohol, or "temperance," movements started. These encouraged people to stop drinking altogether and become teetotalers. Similar movements in the U.S. and Scandinavia led to the total prohibition of alcohol during the 1920s and early 1930s. Although the temperance movement achieved some success, many people started to make their own alcohol and some people set up organizations to import and sell it illegally on a black market.

Advertisements warn people of the risks to health and may stop some people from drinking. Films on television and at the movies can be effective, but health education programs probably have the greatest impact, particularly on young people. Such programs may have been responsible for the slight drop in consumption of alcohol seen in the U.S., Canada, and Australia in the early 1980s.

ALCOHOL

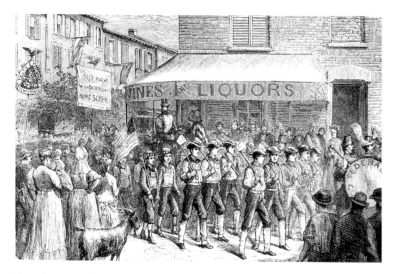

Drunkenness has been a social problem for many years. In the nineteenth century there was a strong "temperance" movement against alcohol. This print is of a temperance march held in Philadelphia in 1876.

What are we drinking?

Some countries have a national preference for one type of alcoholic drink or another. The French and Italians drink wine, and the Soviets drink vodka. Americans, Canadians, Britains, and Australians are beer drinkers. In the U.S. cider, a mild alcoholic apple wine, was the most common drink until the early nineteenth century. It was produced in abundance from the orchards of New England and New York. The popularity of beer emerged after the Civil War, when America's taste for beer grew as the millions of German and middle-European immigrants who entered this country at that time brought their tastes and customs with them.

To traditionally beer-drinking countries such as Germany, there is now a trend toward the drinking of wine and spirits. Wine-drinking countries such as France and Hungary report the increased consumption of beer and spirits. There has also been a move away from traditionally made beverages to commercially produced drinks. For example, in Japan the sales of *sake,* a rice wine, have dropped, and beer and whiskey are being consumed instead. In Mexico, *pulque,* which is made from cactus juice, is now being replaced by beer.

The consumer

Today, the pattern of drinking is changing. People are beginning to drink at an earlier age. Research indicates that young people take their first drink at age 12; in the 1940s and 1950s the age was 13 or 14. Teenage drinking is considered a major problem in some countries and sometimes there are government-sponsored health education courses available. Women are drinking more than before. Cirrhosis of the liver, which is caused by heavy drinking, used to be five times more common in men than women. Now it is only twice as common for a man to suffer from cirrhosis of the liver.

> "It wasn't until I kept an alcohol diary, filling it in every time I had a drink, that I realized just how much I was drinking."

Many people are unaware of the damage that alcohol can do to them. Some family doctors now routinely take a "drinking history" from their patients. This gives them an opportunity to talk about alcohol and the harm it can do to the body and the mind.

It is recommended that:

Parents teach their children the risks of alcohol use.
Young people say no to alcohol.
Children learn that beer and wine coolers contain alcohol and are different from soft drinks.
The limit of safe drinking for adults is $1\frac{1}{2}$ ounces of alcohol per day. That equals the amount of alcohol contained in two bottles of beer, two glasses of wine, or two $1\frac{1}{4}$ ounce drinks of 100-proof whiskey.
Adults should sip rather than gulp drinks.
Dilute drinks with ice cubes or soda.
Avoid alcohol on an empty stomach.
Avoid alcohol when lonely, depressed, sad, or angry.

Jenny, who is 25 and works in a public relations firm, kept an alcohol diary and surprised herself with the results: "It wasn't until I kept an alcohol diary, filling it in every time I had a drink, that I realized just how much I was drinking each week."

27

ALCOHOL

Jenny's diary

Monday

LUNCH	DINNER	EVENING
CLIENTS	AT HOME	WITH FRIENDS
2 GLASSES	1 GLASS WINE	1 GIN AND TONIC

Tuesday

BOB TOOK ME OUT TO DINNER
3 GLASSES WINE

Wednesday

LUNCH	DINNER
CLIENTS	STAYED AT HOME
2 GLASSES	1 BEER

Thursday

MADE SUPPER FOR PARENTS   2 GLASSES OF WINE

Friday

WORKED LATE. MY BOSS BROUGHT IN SUPPER
3 GLASSES OF WINE

Saturday

LUNCH	EVENING
2 BEERS	PARTY - 4 GLASSES GIN AND TONIC

Sunday

LUNCH	DINNER
2 GLASSES OF WINE	1 BEER

Jenny drank 24 units of alcohol, ten drinks more than is considered safe for her health.

5

A UNIVERSAL EXPERIENCE

Most cultures do sanction the use of at least one mind-altering chemical, such as alcohol. It is as though people need to escape from the reality of everyday life and so seek out drugs that help them to do this.

Most societies recognize this need and develop a drug that is socially acceptable for their members to take. The natives in Siberia take the toadstool *Amanita,* and local people in Peru and Colombia chew coca leaves for their stimulating effect. Alcohol is one of the most popular drugs in the world and is consumed in many countries.

However, few societies allow their members to take drugs without some legal sanctions. Usually drug-taking is bound by strict codes and customs. In Central America, the Indians used the drug *peyote,* derived from the cactus plant, to help them have visions during religious ceremonies. The drug is rarely taken at other times.

> *Few societies allow their members to take drugs without some legal sanctions.*

The drinking of alcohol is also "organized." Each country has its own way of controlling consumption. Several countries have licensing laws that control the opening hours of places where alcohol is sold. The way that a bar or club is run is in itself another method by which alcohol consumption is controlled. People socialize in clubs and bars. If there is a large group, there is a tendency for everyone to continue drinking until the bar closes.

Emmons School Discovery Center **29**

ALCOHOL

In Mediterranean countries such as France, Italy, and Spain, it is customary to drink wine with meals. There is a wide variation in the way that different countries and cultures control alcohol consumption.

Latin America

Before the arrival of the Spanish conquerors in the 1500s, the native South Americans drank locally brewed alcohol on special days such as harvest festivals, weddings, and burials. It was expected that people would become intoxicated on these holy days but never drunk. They were punished if they drank too much, and solitary drinking was discouraged. A fermented drink called *chicha* made from oats, apples, strawberries, and corn, and pulque made from the juice of the agave cactus were drunk. Neither of these drinks contained much alcohol.

The Spaniards brought with them more intoxicating drinks such as wine and spirits. Under the influence of the Spanish invaders, many customs changed, including the pattern of alcohol consumption. Indeed, alcohol was used against the native peoples, and there are sad stories about natives signing away their rights to land when drunk.

Quechua Indians from Cuzco drinking *chicha*.

As Indians moved to the cities, their drinking became one way of escaping from the reality of their lives — the poor housing, unemployment, poverty. Solitary drinking became more common, and today heavy drinking is a problem in the slum areas around cities. Alcohol is relatively cheap, and there has been a trend toward beer drinking, although this is low when compared to other countries.

> *. . . their drinking became one way of escaping from the reality of their lives — the poor housing, unemployment, poverty.*

In Latin American countries, drinking is considered to be a sign of manhood. It takes place both at home and in bars. It is rude not to accept a drink and impolite not to offer one. Women do not drink in public, while babies and young children are often given alcohol, such as pulque, mixed in with their food because it is considered to be nutritious. In Venezuela, the law forbids more than one shop per 1,000 inhabitants from selling alcohol, but the law is not obeyed.

Japan

In the international table of drinkers by country, Japan comes very near the bottom. The vast majority of Japanese people do not drink alcohol at the table or on a regular daily basis.

In the past, alcohol played a part in the life of the Japanese peasant. The rice-growing farmer, who was not busy during the cold part of the year, would ferment some of the previous years's harvest to produce sake. A priest would be called in to bless certain stages of the brewing process and the resulting drink was often used at religious ceremonies. Today, less sake (rice wine) is consumed as it is expensive compared to other drinks. Little wine is drunk in Japan, but beer is popular. For the more affluent, whiskey is a treat.

Most drinking in Japan is conducted by men in groups. Drinking is a social activity; the men drink together for company and companionship, often after work before returning home. As women become more independent, they too are starting to drink, but there is still a high percentage of Japanese women who have never tasted alcohol.

ALCOHOL

The Japanese do not drink much alcohol but they sometimes drink wine called *sake,* which is fermented from rice. Sake is traditionally served heated.

The Japanese are tolerant about alcohol except when it comes to drinking and driving, and drinking by young people. Both the driver who is over the limit *and* the person who gave the driver alcohol, for example the bartender, are liable for prosecution. A public health poster in Japan reads "Travelers should not be intoxicated when using the train." Young people under the age of 20 are not allowed to buy or drink alcohol.

A public health poster in Japan reads "Travelers should not be intoxicated when using the train."

Africa

Alcohol has been used in Africa for centuries. Beer brewed from cereals and bananas, and wine made from various fruits were drunk in the villages to honor special occasions such as the harvest. Certain business deals or family events such as the birth of a child would be celebrated with a drink, and a bride was paid for by her bridegroom in beer.

Drinking in Africa was a social activity that was strictly controlled. Sometimes only older people were allowed to drink and the traditionally made drinks contained little alcohol. However, drinking enough of any alcoholic beverage can result in drunkenness. Drinking was generally a group activity and in Kenya it was traditional to drink beer from a central vat using a straw. The Zambian language has no word for alcoholism.

> *However, drinking enough of any alcoholic beverage can result in drunkenness.*

However, when European colonizers arrived, alcohol was used as a form of payment. Slaves, precious metals, and oil were paid for in alcohol, and there were factories set up in Europe just to produce cheap alcoholic drinks that could be used to trade. Africans who were in close contact with Europeans also acquired the habit of drinking alcohol with

Before Europeans came to Africa there was very little drinking of alcohol. Now it is available everywhere and even sold on trains.

ALCOHOL

meals. Soon the sale of alcohol and the import taxes on alcohol became crucial to the economy of a colony.

Today, many African countries have abolished restrictions on the sale of alcohol. As a result, there has been an increase in the consumption of imported drinks. Unfortunately, there has also been an increase in the number of people who are reported drunk, and productivity in the work place has been badly affected.

6

ALCOHOL AND YOU

When an alcoholic drink is taken, what effect does it have on the body and brain? This is not an easy question to answer because it depends on the age, sex, and size of the drinker as well as on the type of drink and what the drinker has recently eaten. All these things affect the rate of absorption of alcohol into the bloodstream and how quickly the drinker becomes intoxicated.

Babies and young children feel the effects of even a tiny amount of alcohol. They are small, so only a little alcohol will make them drunk, and their bodies are not used to getting rid of it. Elderly people often find they are unable to drink the same quantities as they did when younger. The liver, which is responsible for breaking down the alcohol in the body, becomes less efficient with age.

> *Babies and young children feel the effects of even a tiny amount of alcohol.*

Women are more easily affected by alcohol than men. There are several reasons for this, but the single most important reason is that most men produce specific stomach enzymes that most women lack. These enzymes begin digesting alcohol before it hits the bloodstream. Another factor to consider is that women may retain less water in their bodies than men so there may be less water in which to dilute the alcohol. Size is a factor, too. Most women are smaller than most men. A big man can drink more than a woman or a small man and not feel or behave as though he is drunk. The larger man simply has a bigger body in which to absorb the alcohol.

ALCOHOL

This child is not drinking alcohol but she is learning that alcohol is socially acceptable. In some countries there are laws that prevent children from drinking because it is very harmful to them.

When alcohol is swallowed, it flows into the stomach. Alcohol is quickly absorbed into the bloodstream from the stomach, particularly if the stomach is empty. If a large meal has just been eaten, absorption of alcohol is only half as fast. This means that a person who has not eaten for several hours should always have a snack before they have a drink.

Alcohol is even carried to an embryo through the placenta, so pregnant women simply should not drink.

Processing the alcohol

Alcohol is carried from the stomach and the intestine to every tissue in the body by blood. Alcohol is even carried to an embryo through the placenta, so pregnant women simply should not drink. Women who drink during pregnancy risk delivering babies with irreversible abnormalities, which is called fetal alcohol syndrome (FAS). Babies may be born mentally retarded. FAS is completely preventable.

The body eliminates alcohol in several ways. Some escapes through the lungs or is passed out in the urine, but most of it is broken down by the liver. This takes time. The liver can only deal with .5 ounces of alcohol an hour, that is, slightly less than two-thirds of a beer or just under a glass of wine. This is why a heavy drinker will wake up and still feel the effects of alcohol the morning after. He or she would not be fit to drive.

The liver can only break down 2.8 ounces of alcohol in a 24-hour period in a man, and 1.4 ounces in a woman. This is the equivalent of just over a bottle of wine for a man and half as much for a woman. Asking the liver to do this in one day is unlikely to cause major health problems, but if large amounts of alcohol are consumed every day, the liver never gets a rest. This is why alcohol-free days are so important.

> *The brain simply does not work as well, and the drinker may find it hard to remember details or to talk clearly.*

Alcohol has two immediate effects on the body. It causes the blood vessels in the skin to open, making the drinker flush and feel warm. It also makes the body pass urine. This can make the body low on water, or dehydrated. Alcohol also stops the absorption of several vitamins, including vitamins B and C. This means that certain parts of the body, such as the liver, brain, and skin, cannot work properly and the drinker is at greater risk of infection than normal.

A "hangover" occurs following heavy consumption of alcohol. Usually the person feels tired, sick, dizzy, has a headache, and may feel shaky. One cause of these symptoms is dehydration, caused by a disruption of body fluids. The shaky feelings are due to the depressing effect that alcohol has on the nervous system. As the blood alcohol level falls, the nerves in the body overreact. There is no "cure" for a hangover. Coffee, tomato juice, vitamins, or more alcohol won't help. The body needs time to rid itself of the alcohol that has been consumed.

Alcohol and the brain

The brain is more likely to be affected by alcohol than any other part of the body. How much it is affected depends on the amount of alcohol in the bloodstream and how quickly it reaches the brain.

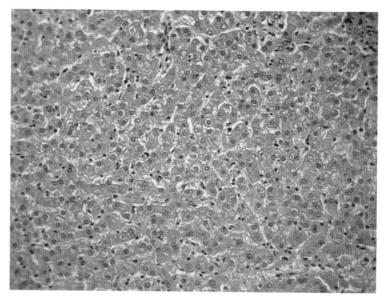

A section from a healthy human liver showing the even distribution of liver cells, which help to get rid of alcohol.

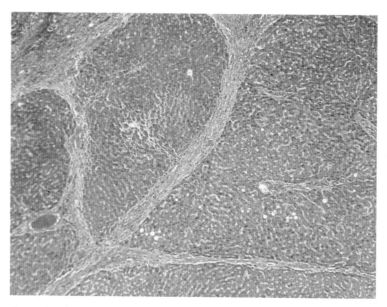

A section from a diseased human liver showing cirrhosis, which is structural damage to the cells often caused by excessive alcohol intake.

After one or two drinks, the drinker feels happier and more carefree. As drinking continues, it may be more difficult to undertake certain tasks that require coordination, such as driving. The brain simply does not work as well, and the drinker may find it hard to remember details or to talk clearly. With heavy drinking, the person's emotions become unpredictable and they are described as "drunk." Finally, if drinking continues, confusion, coma, and eventually even death can follow.

It is clear that over a period of time the brain becomes used to alcohol. While a bottle of whiskey may kill a 17-year-old boy or girl who have not had alcohol before, the 45-year-old man who has been drinking heavily for years will only feel badly hungover in the morning. However, the brain that is exposed to high levels of alcohol over a long period is permanently damaged. In this situation, brain cells shrink and die at a faster rate than normal.

Alcohol and health

A still-debated issue is whether moderate drinking may protect against heart disease. Heart disease results when the blood vessels in the heart, the coronary arteries, become clogged up with fatty deposits. A diet that is rich in fat encourages these fatty deposits to form. It may be that a little alcohol makes the coronary arteries relax and open up, and delays the clogging process. A recent Harvard public-health school study supports this theory.

> *Heavy alcohol intake increases the risk of liver damage, brain damage, high blood pressure, and strokes.*

Alcohol in excess *is* bad for health and can kill. A heavy intake of alcohol increases the risk of liver damage, brain damage, high blood pressure, and strokes. There is some evidence that moderate amounts of alcohol increase the risk of breast cancer in women, although it is not understood why. Alcohol-related causes were responsible for an average of 300 deaths each day in 1987.

ALCOHOL

Alcohol, like any other drug, is addictive. This means that when the effects of a lot of drinking have worn off, the drinker craves more alcohol. Alcoholics will often put everything at risk to satisfy their addiction — their health, their work, and relationships with friends and family.

7

$\triangledown$

ALCOHOLISM

We are all dependent on different things. Some people cannot start the day happily without a cup of coffee, some must be in a certain position to get to sleep, while others do not feel comfortable unless their surroundings are nice and neat. As long as these "addictions" do not start to rule a person's life, they do not present a problem. Drinking alcohol is a pleasure, but when it becomes more important than other things in life, it has gotten out of control.

Alcohol, like any other drug, is addictive. The image of the alcoholic is that of a down-and-outer who lives on the street, begging for money to buy more liquor. There are some alcoholics who live this way, but there are many more who have jobs, homes, and families.

There is no simple method of defining an alcoholic. Alcoholism is not judged simply on how much someone drinks, but rather what effect the alcohol has on that particular person. Drinking large quantities of alcohol is always dangerous. Even if a person says that they feel fine, a doctor will advise them to cut down to a lower level of consumption so that they do not start to depend on alcohol.

Alcohol is not highly addictive. Many people drink without becoming dependent on alcohol. However, in a sense, that is why alcohol is dangerous. It is easy to drink without realizing that it can become a habit.

Watching for clues

A person who is addicted to alcohol will organize his or her life around their habit. For example, Peter was used to having a drink at lunchtime and, though it was his daughter Phoebe's

41

ALCOHOL

Sometimes alcoholics lose their homes, jobs, and families because of their drinking.

birthday, he could not miss that drink to go and buy her a present. He would also stop at a local bar on the way home from work. "But I could easily not have a drink then," he would tell friends. One day his boss asked him to stay late at work. Peter became irritable and anxious and had to leave the office to go and buy two cans of beer. He drank them quickly in the washroom and then felt better. Peter's addiction was having a bad effect on his work and his family, but he was unable to see or to face up to the problems his dependence on alcohol was causing.

> "I only drink beer and I never get drunk, so how could I be a problem drinker?"

The person who seems to be able to drink a lot without showing any bad effects is also in danger. Sometimes a person will boast he or she can drink amounts of alcohol that would make another person intoxicated: "I only drink beer and I never get drunk, so how could I be a problem drinker? Come on, you have to be drinking a bottle of whiskey a day to be an alcoholic!" This, they claim, shows they are in control of the amount of alcohol they are consuming. What it actually means is that they are becoming dependent on the drug.

In the later stages of alcoholism, a drinker may suddenly find that he or she can no longer pretend that their drinking does not affect them. The liver cannot deal with the alcohol as efficiently as it did before, and the brain has lost its ability to cope with high levels of alcohol.

> *Usually, alcoholics are secretive and clever when they are drinking.*

As alcohol drains from the body, withdrawal symptoms such as shaking, sweatiness, nausea, poor sleep, and mood changes are also the danger signs of heavy drinking. Although people initially drink to feel good, heavy drinkers will probably need to drink to stop themselves from feeling bad.

It is also a bad sign when drinkers start to lie about how much they drink. Usually, alcoholics are secretive and clever when they are drinking. Sally kept a bottle hidden in her car and one at work, and used breath fresheners to disguise the smell of alcohol. When a friend told Sally she thought that she was drinking too much, Sally got furious and told her to mind her own business.

What makes someone an alcoholic?

There is no actual cause of alcoholism. A person may drink too much because they are unhappy or lonely, because they have too much or too little money, because they are bored or cannot cope with pressure, because they have personality problems, or because they are influenced by the example of someone close to them, like their father or mother.

A common question is "My dad's an alcoholic. Does that mean I can never have a drink because I'll turn into an alcoholic, too?" There is a minority of people who actually inherit a tendency to become alcoholic. Their bodies lack a particular set of chemicals. This lack makes them very sensitive to alcohol and their bodies cannot break it down as efficiently as other people's. However, there is no simple formula that makes someone an alcoholic; there are many factors involved in the development of an addiction.

ALCOHOL

Bartenders are more likely to become alcoholics than people in other jobs.

It usually takes several years for alcohol dependence to set in. The reported increase in teenage drinking leads people to think that there will be an increase in young alcoholics. Moreover, people in certain job categories, especially those who are away from home a lot and have the use of expense accounts, such as salespeople or performers, have more tendency to become alcoholics. Also prone to drinking are people who have stressful occupations — company executives, law enforcement officers, and military personnel.

The impact of alcoholism

Alcoholism has effects other than physical ones on a drinker. Social and emotional problems are common, and the result is a little like a whirlpool, dragging family, friends, and employers into it and destroying the relationships with them.

Tom lost his job through drunkenness and because he always needed time off to sober up. His wife, Sandra, threw him out and his friends found Tom difficult to talk to. He missed his family and got lonely so he drank and became more ill. It is important to realize that the alcoholic may have several problems all at once. Encouraging alcoholics to give up liquor is not going to work if they are not also encouraged to try to solve the problems that may have led them to drink heavily in the first place.

Treatment

Often, a drinker needs medical help to return to living a normal life. The process of giving up alcohol or, "drying out," is a hard, tough one, and the drinker has to go into a hospital or a special clinic. Doctors usually prescribe tranquilizers for a patient to combat anxiety and the fits that usually occur.

> *The process of giving up alcohol, or "drying out," is a hard, tough one.*

If a drinker's physical condition is poor, he or she will need to build up the body with vitamins and good food. There may also be other problems such as liver or stomach complaints, which the doctor can treat. Sometimes doctors prescribe *antabuse,* a drug that interacts with alcohol to make a person vomit if they drink alcohol.

Dealing with the physical recovery of an alcoholic is only the beginning. The drinker must then learn a whole new way of life that does not rely on drink. Many people in the U.S. and in Europe join an organization called Alcoholics Anonymous. The organization gives them invaluable contact with other people who have overcome alcohol problems. Relatives can join Al-Anon or Al-Ateen. In these organizations they learn how to help their family member give up alcohol and to understand the difficulties the ex-alcoholic is going through.

Treatment for alcoholism is about 60 percent successful if the person wants to give up drink. Some experts think that before treatment starts it is essential that the drinker admit to himself or herself that they have a problem: "I wake with the shakes in the morning and need a drink before I leave the house. I keep a bottle in my desk drawer and take a few nips throughout the day and I stop at a bar on the way home. I couldn't cope without it." No one can make another person stop drinking. The desire to change has to come from the drinker who has finally accepted that alcohol is making his or her life miserable and unproductive.

> *The desire to change has to come from the drinker who has finally accepted that alcohol is making his life miserable and unproductive.*

Some centers can deal with alcoholics who are less motivated, and help them in a time of crisis. Treatment is only 20 to 30 percent successful with these drinkers. Only 20 percent of alcoholics go to professional agencies for help and advice.

One of the ways used to get people to control their alcohol problem is group therapy where people can talk about their difficulties.

8

YOUNG PEOPLE
AND ALCOHOL

Alcohol is a drug used by many young people. Studies from around the developed world suggest that the number of young people who adopt drinking as a habit is growing. Other studies conclude that drinking among young people has not changed much in forty years. It is sometimes difficult for researchers to separate fact from opinion.

Among American high school seniors, it is reported that about 4 percent drink daily and 92 percent have tried alcohol. This rate is high despite the fact that they are too young to buy alcohol. Alcohol is the number one drug problem among young people in America. In Great Britain, alcohol consumption among teenagers has reportedly doubled in the period 1949 to 1979. Since then it has been tailing off slightly.

> . . . *many people finally realized that alcohol is the most widely used drug among teenagers — and the rest of the population.*

This world trend in early drinking sparked off public debates in many countries. Many parents worried that there was an epidemic of teenage drinkers. Since the legal drinking age in the U.S. is twenty-one, many feel that any use of alcohol among people younger than the legal age is an abuse. In one way, the increased public awareness of alcohol was good, for many people finally realized that alcohol is the most widely used drug among teenagers — and the rest of the population.

However, the World Health Organization produced a report on young people and alcohol that concluded that, while there was some cause for concern about the amount of alcohol that

ALCOHOL

Young fans drinking at soccer games have caused a lot of problems because they become very aggressive and violent, which has led to tragedy in the U.K.

young people are consuming, the extent of the problem was often exaggerated. The report stressed the importance of identifying the small number of teenagers who were drinking excessively so that help could be offered to them.

The teenage drinking problem

Alcohol is easily obtained by young people. It is cheaper in real terms today than it has ever been before, and young people have more money in their pockets than their parents or grandparents did. Alcohol is also more widely available and sold from a great variety of outlets. Many young people follow the example of their parents and other adults — adults over 21 are also drinking more than ever before. It is not surprising that many teenagers assume that it is all right if they drink.

There are other factors that influence the decision to drink. Advertisements for alcohol are persuasive. Good-looking young people appear in the advertisements, which are often set in exotic locations. These ads suggest that the person who drinks is glamorous, sophisticated, and successful in their working lives and with the opposite sex. In many countries, the advertising of alcoholic drinks on television and at the movies is controlled or even banned.

For some young people, the final years at school are traumatic. There are examinations to pass and decisions to be made about a future job, training, or college. Alcohol can be a comfort and a prop. If the future looks uncertain or bleak, having a drink can drive away the fears and doubts, if only for a short time.

> *Advertisements . . . suggest that the person who drinks is glamorous, sophisticated, and successful in their working lives and with the opposite sex.*

This Spanish advertisement for alcohol shows a young, sophisticated couple to create the image wanted for the product.

ALCOHOL

Boys and girls show different drinking patterns. A boy will tend to drink in the company of other boys. There may be pressure on him to prove his manhood by drinking in excess and binge drinking is common. If a boy is introduced to alcohol by his parents, they will usually offer it to him at an earlier age than his sisters. Girls usually drink with their boyfriends, often on weekends and when they have something to celebrate. It used to be that boys drank much more than girls but the gap has been closing in recent years.

Drinking patterns

Most children are first given alcohol by their parents. In Mediterranean countries, drinking is associated with family life and children will be offered alcohol with the meal. In the U.S. and the U.K., where alcohol is part of a social life, a child may be given a sip when the family is entertaining friends.

However, as children enter their teens, many start to drink with friends. Teenagers tend to drink heavily at parties rather than on a regular basis. According to research done in France, teenagers in paid employment drink more than their contemporaries who are students and have no money. A similar pattern is seen in Germany and Poland. It is as though the workers adopt the drinking habits of their elders. However, young people who are unemployed also tend to drink heavily.

The dangers of alcohol

What many people fail to realize is that drinking in excess can kill. A bottle of whiskey, for example, can send a person into a coma. The alcohol slows down or depresses the brain, and breathing stops. Also, the person may vomit and, because they are unconscious, breathe in vomit and choke to death.

> What many people fail to realize is that drinking in excess can kill. A bottle of whiskey . . . can send a person into a coma.

Alcohol is bad for the brain and body if taken in excessive amounts, but a young drinker will soon recover good health if the drinking stops. In the long term, it is not ill-health that is the major problem for the young drinker, but the effect that alcohol

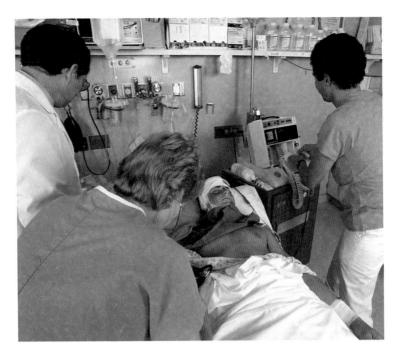

Alcohol causes a lot of accidents both at home, work, and in the street. Pedestrians who have been drinking are more likely to be careless when crossing the street.

has on behavior. Drinking makes someone more accident-prone and accidents are the major cause of death among young people.

More than 800 youngsters 14 and below and more than 8,000 15– to 24-year-olds died in alcohol-related highway accidents in 1988. Even small amounts of alcohol affect the coordination of people of all ages. They become clumsier and their reaction time to unexpected events is slower than normal. This is especially true when driving and, with the added false sense of confidence that alcohol also gives, is the cause of many accidents. It seems that young people are particularly likely to be affected by low levels of alcohol. Inexperienced drinkers have a lower tolerance for alcohol and their judgment is impaired by taking only small amounts.

Drinking also increases the risk of injury from other accidents. Research done in Helsinki, Finland, shows that a high blood level of alcohol is a common cause of accidental falls, for example, by pedestrians in the street. Accidents in the home and at work are more likely to happen when someone has been drinking.

There is a link, too, between alcohol and violence. Alcohol does not cause violence, but it may make the problem worse. A study in Boston, Massachusetts, found that over half of a group of injured people treated after a fight had been drinking, and available figures show that over half the offenders involved in rape, murder, and assault had been drinking. The fact that a person's judgment has been impaired by drinking can lead to many problems for young people, including unwanted pregnancy, and particularly today the possibility of contracting AIDS.

There is also a link between drinking and drug-taking. In Belgium, research has found that alcohol is often taken with marijuana and heroin, and this pattern is repeated in many other countries. It is as though the young person who is willing to risk drinking in large amounts is also the kind of person who will experiment with other drugs.

The good news is that there is no evidence that early heavy drinking always leads to alcoholism in later life. However, habits established early on in life can be very difficult to break.

Health education

Moderate drinking can be a pleasure. Taking wine with a meal brings out the flavor of food, and getting together with friends over a beer is a popular way to socialize. It is important, however, that people understand how to drink.

> *Taking wine with a meal brings out the flavor of food, and getting together with friends over a beer is a popular way to socialize.*

For example, drinking on an empty stomach can make you sick and the alcohol is much more quickly absorbed into the body. If alcoholic drinks are not alternated with nonalcoholic drinks, a person may likely wake up the next morning with a hangover.

There are easy guidelines to sensible drinking. Drinking a glass of wine when at a party or when visiting family or friends is not going to do serious harm to most people. Feel free to refrain from alcohol altogether. Sparkling water or a diet soft drink, coffee or tea, are healthier, low calorie, and fashionable alternatives.

People of every age must learn how to control alcohol — not let it control them.

9

COMBATING ABUSE

In most countries of the world, alcohol is freely available. Yet within each country, depending on culture and custom, there are different rules governing who, where, and when people can consume alcohol. There are rules that govern and limit the amount of alcohol that, for example, a vehicle driver can drink, and taxes have to be paid on every bottle of alcohol that is bought.

These taxes on alcohol raise a lot of money for a government. This means that governments often have a great interest in promoting the sale of alcohol, if only indirectly, because of the revenue they gain from the taxes.

Alcohol is a big profit-making product. The highest tax is made on a bottle of spirits, while less tax is charged on beer or wine. In the U.S., there is a federal tax and, depending on the state, a state tax on alcohol. In Australia, the tax on beer is directly linked to inflation, or rises in the cost of living, and

> *Health campaigners argue that, if governments want to control alcohol abuse, they should raise taxes on alcohol.*

therefore increases in line with the rate of inflation. In Germany there is no tax on wine, while in other European countries wine tax varies between nothing and very little.

Some groups, like the alcoholic beverage industry, think governments charge too much in taxes on liquor. Health campaigners, on the other hand, think alcohol should be more expensive. They say there is a link between alcohol consumption and the cost of alcohol. If it costs people a lot to

DUTY FREE SHOP

In most countries there are customs duties and taxes on alcohol. This earns a lot of revenue for the government. At airports, duty-free alcohol for export can be bought with less or no tax.

drink, fewer will do it in excess. Health campaigners argue that, if governments want to control alcohol abuse, they should raise taxes on alcohol. The alcohol industry does not agree with this. In a free society, they argue, people should be allowed to use their money as they wish. Moderate drinkers would be unfairly penalized if taxes were raised.

In the U.S. the legal age for drinking is 21 and young people have to present identification cards to prove their age. This is a recent development. In the 1960s, the voting age was reduced to 18 and, soon after that, young men and women of 18 were also allowed to drink. However, research suggested the lower legal age for drinking led to a rise in the number of people killed on the roads.

In 1980, a thirteen-year-old girl was killed by a drunk driver on a highway in Sacramento, California. The driver had been charged five times previously with drunk driving. The girl's mother, Candy Lightner, began what was to be an enormously successful grass-roots movement called Mothers Against Drunk Driving (MADD) to protest lax laws against drunk drivers. MADD is credited with bringing the problem of drunk driving to the attention of the public and thus changing the public's views on how to deal with offenders. Since MADD's inception, the legal drinking age was raised to 21 in 1988, and tougher laws and penalties have been enacted against offenders. Soon after MADD, a student organization called Students Against Drunk Driving (SADD) came into being in high schools and on college campuses, with the purpose of enlightening students about the dangers of driving while intoxicated.

Drinking and driving

Driving while intoxicated is dangerous and illegal. The National Council on Alcoholism and Drug Dependence (NCADD) reports that about half of all fatal highway crashes are alcohol related. Statistics show that in 1988 1.8 million arrests were made for drinking and driving, and 23,352 people died from alcohol-related crashes. One out of every three truck drivers who died in highway accidents had consumed alcohol or other drugs. These are the sobering road statistics. But alcohol abuse contributes to millions of nonfatal injuries and thousands of fatal injuries at home, play, or in public places off the highways. Alcohol causes almost half of all injuries and

Since MADD's inception . . . tougher laws and penalties have been enacted against offenders.

fatalities in the workplace, and alcohol contributes to injury and death in the air, in the water, and on railroad tracks.

The NCADD also reports that 54 percent of the offenders convicted of violent crimes had consumed alcohol prior to the crime. On college campuses, more than half of the students who confess to committing violent crimes were under the influence of alcohol or another drug, and more than half of the victims of violent crimes on campus had used alcohol or another drug at the time they were victimized.

The Surgeon General's Workshop on Drunk Driving recommends banning alcohol advertising and promotions on college campuses. Many college students are under the legal drinking age. The Surgeon General also recommends making driving illegal at a lower blood alcohol level than the one

**YOUR BEST MATE
IS THE ONE
WHO WON'T BUY
YOU A DRINK
IF YOU'RE DRIVING.**

**DRINKING AND DRIVING
WRECKS LIVES.**

Throughout the developed world there have been campaigns to control drinking and driving.

presently acceptable. Any alcohol concentration in the body increases the chance of accidents while driving. The Surgeon General recommends raising federal excise taxes on beer and wine to that of distilled spirits, which would make alcoholic beverages more expensive to buy. Research indicates that if the tax rates by pure alcohol content were equalized on alcoholic beverages, the number of 18- to 20-year olds killed on the roads from 1975 to 1981 would have been reduced by 21 percent.

Each state has its own laws and penalties for those charged with or convicted of drunk driving. If a driver is suspected of driving while intoxicated, almost all states require that he or she submit to a blood alcohol test, usually by breath analysis. In many states, refusing to take the test is considered an

In 1988 1.8 million arrests were made for drinking and driving, and 23,352 people died from alcohol-related crashes.

The breath test is now used routinely at an accident to check whether the driver had been drinking. Its use has helped control drinking and driving in many countries.

admission of guilt and results in automatic license suspension. If convicted of drunk driving, in almost every state, the driver is subjected to a term of imprisonment, a substantial fine, evaluation and possible alcohol treatment, and a mandatory period of license suspension. Those convicted of subsequent drunk driving convictions are subject to substantially enhanced penalties.

Cracking down

Warning labels on some alcoholic beverages advise that "women should not drink alcoholic beverages during pregnancy because of the risk of birth defects" and that "consumption of alcohol impairs the ability of the drinker to drive a car or operate machinery."

In some states, hosts of even private parties are responsible for serving alcohol to guests. Should a guest become visibly intoxicated and subsequently injure a third party, the host may bear some liability for that injury. According to a Gallup-Advertising Age poll, most adults approve of health warnings on alcoholic beverages, and almost half of those polled believe alcohol advertising should be completely banned.

Most developed countries have laws that affect how alcohol is consumed. Laws vary and change according to the culture of the country and to the vigor of pressure groups such as the alcohol industry or health campaigners. Unfortunately, there are unlikely to be many major changes in the approach of governments as long as there is a good income to be earned from taxes on alcohol.

INFORMATION

United States
Al-Anon Family Groups
P.O. Box 862
Midtown Station
New York, NY 10018

Alcoholics Anonymous (A.A.)
15 E. 26th Street Rm 1810
New York, NY 10010

Alcohol Research Information Service
1120 East Oakland Avenue
Lansing, Michigan 48906

Center for Science in the Public Interest
1501 16th Street NW
Washington D.C. 20036

Department of Education
Office of the Secretary
400 Maryland Avenue SW, Room 4181
Washington D.C. 20202

Mothers Against Drunk Driving
511 E. John Carpenter Freeway
Suite 700
Irving, TX 75062

National Clearing House for Alcohol Information
PO Box 2345
Rockville, Maryland 20852

National Council on Alcoholism
12 West 21st Street
New York, New York 10010

Canada
Addiction Research Foundation
33 Russell Street
Toronto, Ontario M5S 251

Alberta Alcohol and Drug Abuse Commission
10909 Jasper Avenue, 7th Floor
Edmonton, Alberta T5J 3M9

INDEX

INDEX

Library of Congress Cataloging-in-Publication Data

Holmes, Pamela.
    Alcohol / written by Pamela Holmes.
      p. cm. — (Drugs — the complete story)
    Includes index.
    Summary: Focuses on alcohol, the most widely used drug in the
world, its role in religion and history, how it is made, the alcohol
industry, advertising, consumption, and abuse.
    ISBN 0-8114-3203-3 — ISBN 0-8114-3206-8 (soft cover)
    1. Alcoholism — Juvenile literature. 2. Drinking of alcoholic
beverages — Juvenile literature. [1. Alcohol. 2. Alcoholism.]
I. Title. II. Series.
HV5066.H65 1991
362.29'2 — dc20   91-30344
                                               CIP AC

Consultants: Kenneth J. Schmidt, Passaic County, N.J., Probation
Dept.; Marilyn Devroye, consultant for Psychiatric Institutes of
America, Washington, DC.

Editors: Margaret Sinclair, Gina Kulch

Cover design by Joyce Spicer

Typeset by Tom Fenton Studio, Neptune, NJ
Printed and bound by Lake Book, Melrose Park, IL

Photographic Credits
Cover: © James Minor, *inset:* © Grant Heilman/Grant Heilmann, Inc.
page 6 J. Allan Cash; 7 Michael Holford; 9 Popperfoto; 11 Teasy/
ZEFA; 12 ZEFA; 13 Rossenbach/ZEFA; 3, 15 ZEFA; 18 Robert
Harding; 20 J. Allan Cash; 21 F. Damon/ZEFA; 24 J. Allan Cash; 26
Mary Evans Picture Library; 30 Tony Morrison/South American
Pictures; 32 Nigel Blyth/Robert Harding; 33 Robert Harding; 36 Janine
Wiedel; 38a & b Science Photo Library; 42 J. Allan Cash; 2, 44 K.
Benser/ZEFA; 46 The Priory Hospitals Group; 48 Sipa Press/Rex
Features; 49 Barnaby's Picture Library; 51 Larry Mulvehill/ Science
Photo Library; 55 Barnaby's Picture Library; 57 Department of
Transport; 3, 58 Metropolitan Police.

Original tex and illustations
© Heinemann Educational Books Ltd. 1991